World War II Midget Submarine

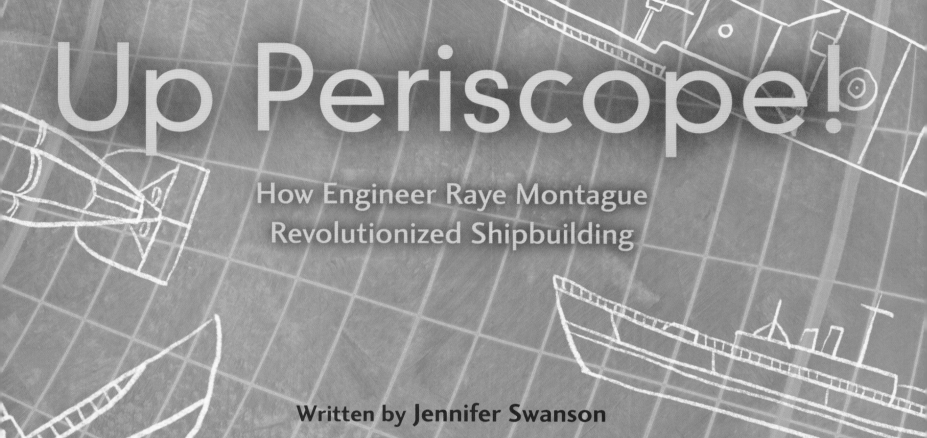

Up Periscope!

How Engineer Raye Montague
Revolutionized Shipbuilding

Written by Jennifer Swanson

Illustrated by Veronica Miller Jamison

L B

Little, Brown and Company
New York   Boston

Seven-year-old Raye Montague's mother had always told her three things:

1. She could learn anything.
2. She could do anything.
3. She could be anything.

But growing up in Little Rock, Arkansas, in the 1940s, life seemed slightly out of focus. The country was at war. Food and money were scarce.

One day in 1943, Raye's grandfather said he wanted to show her something special—a World War II submarine! As Raye climbed down the sub's ladder, she felt curiosity bubble up inside her. It was like stepping into a strange new world.

She put her eye to the periscope. The faraway ships in the harbor suddenly seemed close enough to touch! At that moment, her entire life popped into focus, and Raye knew what she wanted to do. . . .

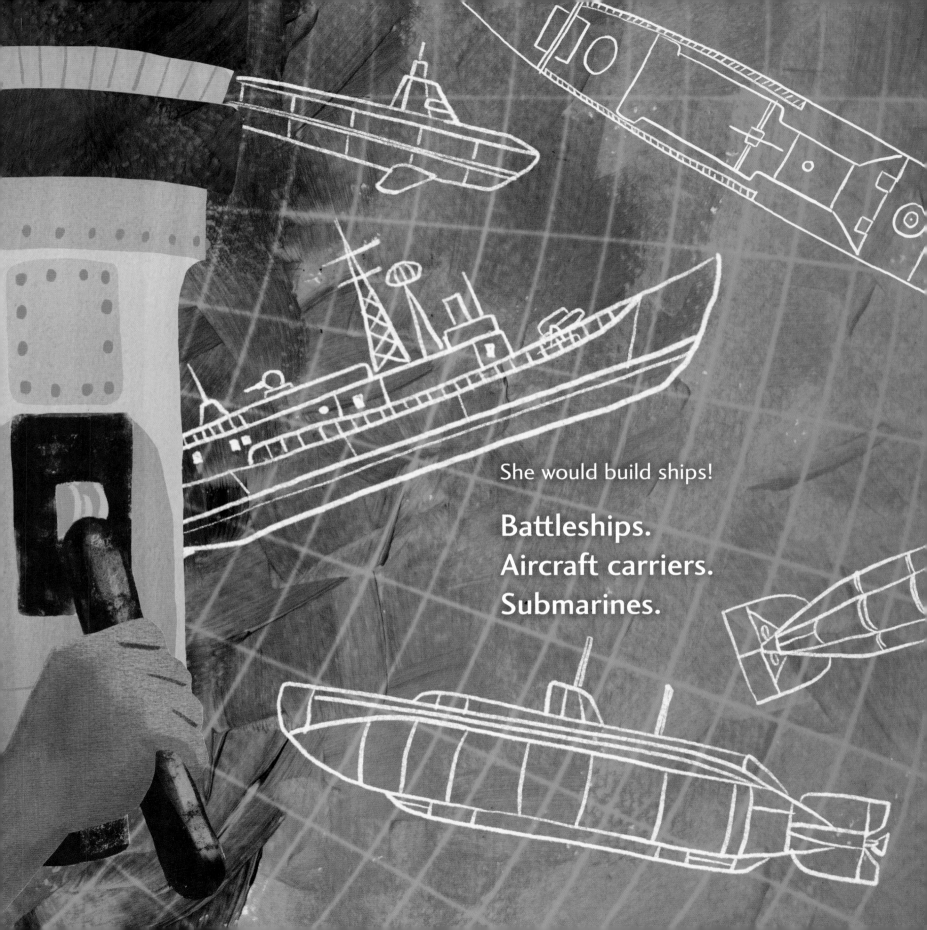

She would build ships!

Battleships.
Aircraft carriers.
Submarines.

Raye asked the naval officer how she could build a submarine like this one. He told her that engineers design submarines, but *she* wouldn't have to worry about doing that.

Raye was confused. Her grandfather explained that girls didn't become engineers—especially not Black girls.

But Raye knew she could

learn anything,

do anything,

and be anything she wanted.

She had a plan.

In high school, Raye tried to take shop, the class where you learned to build things. She was told girls couldn't participate.

So Raye's mother convinced the principal to let Raye in.

Raye's next stop was college. At the time, the engineering department at the University of Arkansas would not allow Black students into their program.

UNIVERSITY OF ARKANSAS
APPLICATION
NAME: Raye Montague
MAJOR: Engineering
AGE: 14
HIGH SCHOOL: Merrill High School
DENIED
GRADUATION: 1956

So Raye went to business school to learn about computers,
still hoping that she would find a way to work as an engineer.

And she did—almost! When Raye graduated, she was hired
by the US Navy. Not as an engineer herself, but as a typist,
working for the male engineers.

Still, Raye was in the right place, and while she waited for her opportunity, she asked questions, took notes, and learned everything she could.

Every day, Raye sat next to the UNIVAC computer, which she wasn't allowed to touch. Only the men trained to run it could do that.

But Raye had a plan: At night, she took computer programming classes to learn how to work the UNIVAC.

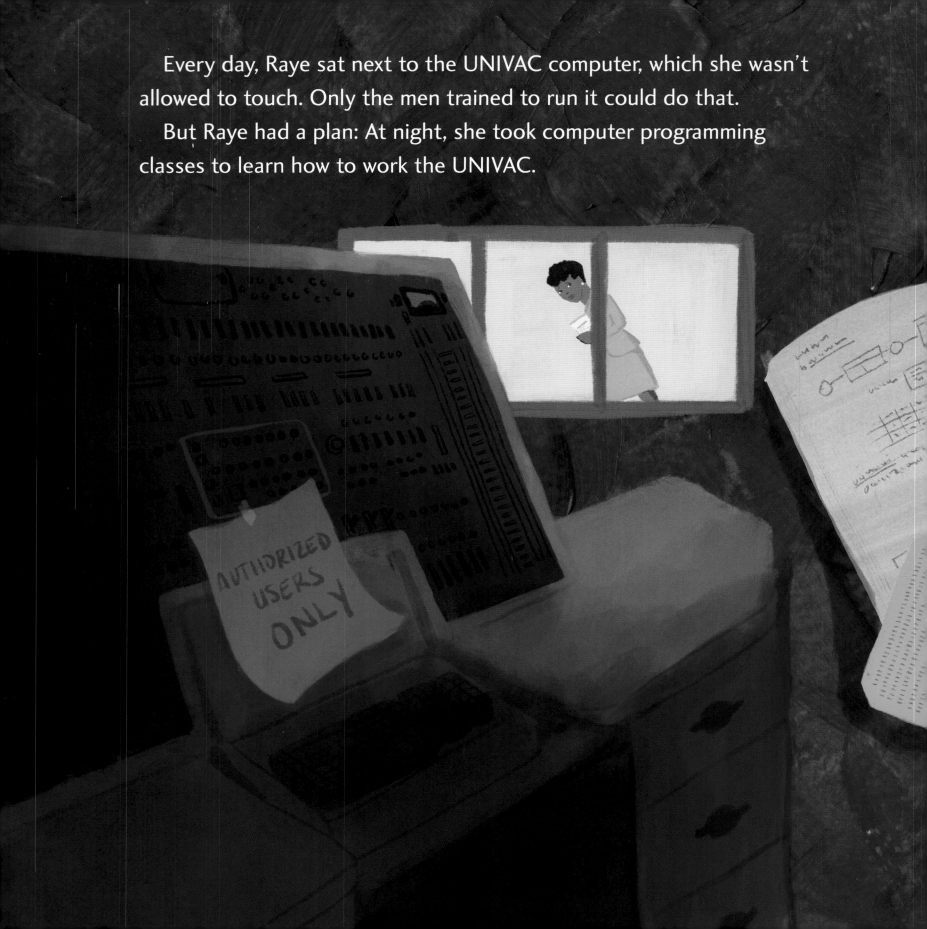

One day, all the men who ran the computer were too sick to come to work. Raye jumped up and took over. Although she'd never touched the machine before, she knew which buttons to push, which levers to flip, and which instructions to type to get the UNIVAC to solve calculations.

Her supervisor was stunned. But Raye did so well that she was eventually promoted to a full-time operator.

It took about fourteen more years, but because of her skill on the UNIVAC system, Raye was finally able to transfer to the Naval Ship Engineering Center.

She was going to design ships!

At the time, ships were designed by hand. It took thousands of hours of work—usually more than two years—by a team of many people to perform all the calculations.

The men in Raye's office didn't like having a woman working with them, especially not a Black woman. They gave her an impossible task: to create a single computer program that could calculate every part of a ship's design.

This had never been done before.
And she had only six months to do it.

RAYE MONTAGUE

DUE 9/1971

1971

MARCH

MARCH

Raye accepted the challenge. She had heard about a team in New York that was using computers for ship design. When she arrived, Raye learned from the team that each computer program did only *one part* of the whole shipbuilding process, and people still had to perform many hours of calculations. No one had any idea how to create a program that could complete all the design steps at once.

But Raye had a plan.

Back at her office, Raye took an old UNIVAC computer completely apart. Over the span of many months, she planned to reprogram each component, then reassemble the computer.

At first, her supervisor would not pay any other employees to help her, and she was not allowed to keep working by herself late at night. So, Raye brought her mother and three-year-old son, David, into the office with her. She taught David how to punch the cards that were needed to create her program.

Eventually, it began to look like Raye's program would succeed, so her supervisor added a few members to her team. This allowed Raye to meet her deadline—and just in time! A special request had come in from President Nixon to see the design of a brand-new navy ship.

Would her program work?

She spent over two days without rest inputting information into the computer. Finally, an exhausted Raye set her new program in motion, watched it for a few hours, and then headed home.

A short time later, she was woken up by a phone call. . . .

Her program worked!

In just eighteen hours and twenty-six minutes, Raye's new program
built the first ever comprehensive ship design.
No one thought a woman could do it.
No one thought a Black woman could do it.
But Raye Montague became the first *person* to do it.

Raye went on to help design some of the largest and most important ships in the navy.

On her last assignment, she finally helped design a navy submarine! She had always known she could

learn anything,
do anything,
and be anything.

And now she could truly call herself
Raye Montague, *engineer.*

More About Raye Montague

Growing up in Arkansas in the 1940s was tough for a young girl with an engineer's mindset. Women weren't supposed to take math and science classes—in fact, they weren't even supposed to *like* math and science. But Raye Montague's mother was a huge influence in her life. She told Raye that there were three strikes against her becoming an engineer: She was female, she was Black, and she would have to attend a segregated school. But Raye didn't let any of that stop her. With her mother's support, Raye tackled every challenge set in her path, and in 1956 she became a third-generation college graduate.

The significance of Raye's achievement might be hard to grasp now since so many of us have a computer at our fingertips. But back in the 1950s and 1960s, the UNIVAC was one of the very first computers ever created. It could only process a thousand words and twelve alphanumeric characters, and couldn't do much by today's standards. In fact, one of Raye's jobs was to figure out how to program the UNIVAC to print CAPITAL letters next to lowercase ones.

Raye's gift was an ability to see the big picture. When she went to New York City to learn shipbuilding programs from Rosenblatt and Sons, she discovered that they had many different programs. The problem was, they didn't all work together. Not one to give up, Raye thought outside the box and figured out how the programs could complement one another. That's how she came up with one overall ship design program.

Raye received many accolades for her accomplishments, such as the Meritorious Civilian Service Award (1972), the navy's third-highest honorary award, and was nominated by the Secretary of the Navy to become the Federal Woman of the Year. After moving on from ship design, Raye became the first female Program Manager of Ships in the US Navy, as well as the first female professional engineer to receive the Society of Manufacturing Engineers Achievement Award (1978) and the National Computer Graphics Association Award for the Advancement of Computer Graphics (1988). Raye was the first female to serve as the secretary on the board of directors for the Numerical Control Society, and was a regular presenter to the US Department of Defense's Joint Chiefs of Staff on computer-related aspects of naval ship design and construction.

After thirty-three momentous years with the navy, Raye retired and was presented with a flag that had been flown over the US Capitol building in her honor. To Raye, this recognition was simply inconceivable. During an interview, she said, "Can you imagine that from a grateful nation?" A flag being flown over the US Capitol for "[a] little girl from Little Rock!"

Raye was a trailblazer for women. Her motto was "You can do anything you want to do provided you are educated. You can be anything you want to be." Always remember that you can learn anything, do anything, and be anything you want, too.

Author's Note

When I first heard about Raye Montague, I felt an overwhelming urge to write her story. I was honored to interview Raye in 2017. Listening to her speaking about her accomplishments was amazing . . . and quite humbling. Raye's passion and sheer determination to succeed in spite of the many obstacles placed in her path because of her race, her sex, and her lack of training came through in every story she told.

After Raye had relayed her inspiring story to me, she made one request. She was very clear on this. The words in the story below were given to me by Raye: *No one thought a woman could do it. No one thought a Black woman could do it. But Raye Montague became the first* person *to do it.*

Raye wanted to be remembered as the first *person* to create a computer program to build a US Navy ship.

As a 1990 graduate of the US Naval Academy (only the eleventh class that included women), I experienced a tiny bit of what Raye went through, struggling to be recognized as the USNA adjusted to life with women on campus. I am proud to have served in the US Navy and hope I broke some small barriers along the way. In the summer of 1989, six years before women were allowed in combat, I was temporarily assigned to an aircraft carrier, the USS *Independence*, with five other women from the Naval Academy. We were able to observe flight operations, participate in signals training, and even for one brief moment *con* (give orders to steer) the ship! (The captain was standing right next to us.) At the time, it may not have seemed like much, but it was a small step toward the future. None of this would have happened without people like Raye and the many other women who came before me making great strides in the fight for equality. I'm honored to share Raye's story!

—Jennifer Swanson

Source Notes • Swanson, Jennifer. Personal interview with Raye Montague, May 30, 2017. • **Select Works Cited** • "Against the Odds: Naval Engineer Raye Montague." Military.com. Member 30298028. March 24, 2017. military.com/video/specialties-and-personnel/engineers/against-the-odds-naval-engineer-raye-montague/5370909632001. • Bashe, C. J. *IBM's Early Computers.* Cambridge, MA: MIT Press, 1986. • Cobb, Steve. "History of Naval Design and Purpose." *The History of Naval Design.* May 1999. gwpda.org/naval/scnavdes.htm. • Faller , Angelita. "Montague Mother and Son Duo Say Education Is the Key to Breaking Barriers." University of Arkansas Little Rock. February 24, 2017. ualr.edu/news-archive/2017/02/24/david-raye-montague-breaking-barriers.
"History and Timeline." Unix. unix.org/what_is_unix/history_timeline.html. • "Memory & Storage | Timeline of Computer History." Computer History Museum. 2017. computerhistory.org/timeline/memory-storage. • O'Neill, Craig, and Michael Buckner. "Raye Montague Broke Barriers as Arkansas' Own 'Hidden Figure.'" KTHV. February 2, 2017. thv11.com/article/news/local/raye-montague-broke-barriers-as-arkansas-own-hidden-figure/91-387386067. •"Raye Montague, a U.S. Navy 'Hidden Figure.'" *Naval Sea Systems Command.* March 24, 2021. navsea.navy.mil/Media/News/SavedNewsModule/Article/2549135/raye-montague-a-us-navy-hidden-figure. •"Records of the Bureau of Ships." National Archives and Records Administration. 2016. archives.gov/research/guide-fed-records/groups/019.html#19.8.5. • "U-505 Submarine." Museum of Science and Industry. November 27, 2017. msichicago.org/explore/whats-here/exhibits/u-505-submarine. • Vicinanzo, Amanda. "'Hidden Figure of U.S. Navy' Raye Montague Speaks at Dahlgren." Fredericksburg.com. *The Free Lance-Star.* April 4, 2017. fredericksburg.com/news/local/king_george/hidden-figure-of-u-s-navy-raye-montague-speaks-at/article_e88759ab-2b49-5d19-8759-91efefb97803.html.

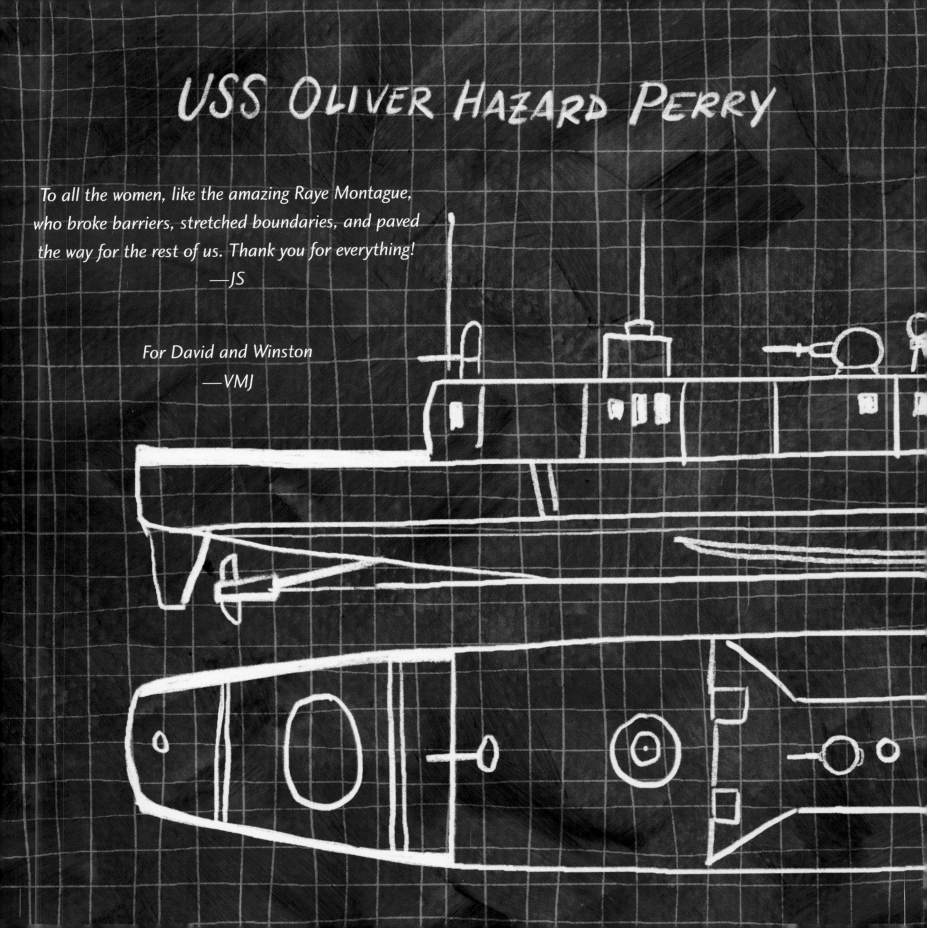

USS Oliver Hazard Perry

To all the women, like the amazing Raye Montague,
who broke barriers, stretched boundaries, and paved
the way for the rest of us. Thank you for everything!
—JS

For David and Winston
—VMJ